THE
SUCCESSFUL
HYBRID
AUTHOR

THE
SUCCESSFUL
HYBRID
AUTHOR

KATLYN DUNCAN

First published January 2023, by Silent Storm Publishing

www.KatlynDuncan.com

Cover designed by 100Covers

eBook ISBN: 9781954559110

Paperback ISBN: 9781954559127

Hardcover ISBN: 9781954559141

Publisher's Note: This work is drawn from the author's experience with publishing, and is meant to inspire and inform writers with tools and strategies to succeed in doing the same. The information in his book should be adopted to each individual's needs and goals for their books. As this book was published in 2023, industry information may change after publication.

Contents

To the incredible editors that I've worked with over the years. You have made me into the author I am today, and I am forever grateful for you.

Why Should You Become a Hybrid Author?

When a writer wants to publish their book, there is a natural divide between going the traditional or independent publishing route. The traditional route involves having an agreement with a publishing house with no upfront costs to the author. Independent publishing typically has the author as the publisher, who pays for all publishing costs.

But you can split your career into both.

You can look at one book project or series with a honed eye and decide to go either route.

How do you do that?

That's what this guide is for.

Being a hybrid author is all about control, and who wouldn't want to run their own career? A hybrid author is an author who publishes both traditionally and independently.

For far too long, traditional publishing houses have ruled many authors' careers, but in this amazing modern age, this doesn't have to be the case anymore.

When I consider being "hybrid", I imagine two catalogs splayed out in front of me.

One of them contains querying methods, how to get an agent, negotiating contracts, publishing with a New York house or a smaller press, networking with other publishing professionals at big literary events, etc.

The other has fresh and innovative marketing methods, release strategies, tactics on how to capitalize on your backlist titles, and more.

With all those possibilities in front of you, you have the power to flip through them, picking what you want from them and molding your author career into one you're happy to live inside for a long time, and be the success you've always dreamed.

My Hybrid Journey

Initial Path to Publication

My journey began with the traditional route of publishing.

In 2012, I signed a contract with a digital-first imprint for a three-book young adult paranormal series. That was without an agent. The first book in my debut series, released June 2013 in eBook. The second and third books came out less than a year later. From 2013-2019, I signed three more contracts, totaling thirteen books traditionally published.

Becoming Hybrid

Throughout those years of publishing, I learned a lot about how to craft a compelling novel, how to be collaborative with a team (with my publisher and while freelance ghostwriting), and what I did or didn't want for my career.

My biggest pain points with traditional publishing were author orphaning and lack of communication, which left me with a lot of self-doubt about my career and made me look for greener pastures. The term "orphaning" refers to editors leaving an imprint or the business for any reason. At most traditional publishers, editors are like project managers for your book, they champion for it in the acquisitions phase, they go through developmental and line edits with you for your manuscript, they oversee the cover creation process, and if you are given a marketing budget, they would be a part of that too. Now, imagine that person, your champion, leaving the publication house or industry altogether. What happens to you?

Since you've signed a contract, it is normal to remain at the imprint when your editor leaves as the publisher assigns you another one. That editor might be amazing and take your book to equal or greater heights than your previous, which I've experienced. Or you become another book an editor must finish to get back to the ones that they had championed for, which I've also experienced.

This isn't a dig at editors, but more at the traditional publishing industry. Droves of editors are leaving the bigger houses because of overwhelm and not enough pay. The trickle-down effect is hitting authors, especially mid-list ones—those that are consistent in getting contracts but aren't making the big money. In the span of publishing my first book and the last novella for the mermaid series, I had worked through seven different editors.

Coupled with the lack of communication, sometimes it took months to get a simple response.

My frustration built up over the years until I was ready to pop.

In 2020, I experienced the worst burnout I ever had and never thought I would write again. The idea of writing books I wasn't super passionate about, during one of the scariest times in so many people's lives, didn't seem all that important.

It wasn't until I reached out to two friends, and we started writing over video chat, that I discovered what I needed was accountability to get my writer-legs back. I started rewriting a book that had been in my mind since 2017 and it felt good to return to what seemed like a simpler time, writing the story that I needed.

When the next contract landed in my inbox, I was so jaded by the traditional publishing experience that I turned it down. If I was going to publish again, they would be books I wanted to write and those that I was more than just proud of. They would become my legacy.

A tremendous shift moved within me. The control of doing what I wanted, not what someone told me.

With that freedom, I started to gain much more confidence about my novel.

I queried that book, interested in getting better deals for myself with an agent. At the same time, the rights reverted to me on my debut paranormal trilogy, so I had an additional three books to publish myself too.

With the process of figuring out what to do with the books, I had a story to share. My debut self-published book *Take Back Your Book: An Author's Guide to Rights Reversion and Publishing On Your Terms* while a mouthful for sure, it is packed with information—while detailing my own journey —on how to get your rights reverted and begin your hybrid author journey

Soon after, I released the second edition of the first book in my paranormal series, *Soul Taken*. It even won an award in 2022!

Between books reverting to me and catching the control-bug, I'm continuing to independently publish for the foreseeable future. I can't say that I have any regrets about the process, and I'm not sure if I started off indie-publishing that I would have felt any more empowered. But that's the beautiful thing about being a hybrid author. No regrets, only forward motion.

What to Expect From This Book

- Honesty: My honest opinions about my hybrid author journey and the ups and downs of it.
- Knowledge: The pros and cons of both traditional and independent book publishing paths, shown through my journey and other successful authors who were gracious enough to share their stories.
- Confidence: Considerations for your career to make the right choices for you and your book.
- Case Studies: If you don't connect with my path, I have four other author's paths to consider for being a hybrid author. Two who started traditional and two who started independent.

Case Studies

When I'm looking for information, I like to search for many different resources. For me, that includes written information, such as articles, and books, along with podcasts and YouTube videos. The main reason for writing this guide is because I didn't find a lot of information out there about hybrid authors. Mostly, I was looking for the process of how to become one and the pros and cons.

For this guide, similar to *Take Back Your Book: An Author's Guide to Rights Reversion and Publishing On Your Terms*, I found so much more information when I reached out to my author network and beyond.

The exciting part for me was interviewing several authors who I admire and putting together more of a case study scenario for you. I wanted to reflect on the conversations, and I hope they are as helpful to you as they were to me.

And as someone who loves video content, I'm offering those full interviews to anyone who reads this book at www. katlynduncan.com/hybrid.

Who Can This Book Help?

The Traditional Author

Starting off here is a great way to get your feet wet. There is no upfront investment for you to publish. You're working with professionals in the field, and you have little responsibility in the production of the book outside of writing and editing.

Considerations for Moving into the Indie Space

Whether you are a debut author or have been publishing for years, learn as much as you can from your editors. If you're lucky, learn from your publicist and marketing teams too. Always strive for more information about your field. Pay attention to how your books are marketed and if you are able (I know, royalty reports are notorious for being difficult to interpret nuances), track what your publishers are doing and see if they have any return. This is the start to taking control and setting yourself up for success when you finally decide to independently publish.

The Independent Author

Overall, this method of publishing is a higher financial risk than the counterpart since you are covering all the upfront costs of publishing. But you also recoup higher percentages of royalties and keep control over your intellectual property. You know how to produce, distribute, and market a book, so you have a unique advantage in this space. Now, you should decide if you're going to move forward with getting an agent and/or which sub-rights you're going to sell to traditional publishers.

Considerations for Moving into the Traditional Space

There are many resources out there, such as Query Tracker and Publishers Marketplace, to help you find your dream agent and/or publisher. It takes work, and you will come up against a lot of resistance, especially in this publishing climate, but you're used to that, right? And when you get that deal, you have a unique advantage of being much more prepared in understanding what rights to give up, and how to exercise them for yourself. This is very important for you since you already have an audience that you can leverage in your deals.

The Unpublished Author

You may be in the position of having your book ready to publish or have an idea and are unsure what you want to do with it once it's completed. What I outline in my book will educate you on the pros and cons of publishing options so you can make informed decisions about your career. I suggest keeping your mind open to all the possibilities. Be prepared to pivot at any moment. Because, as this book suggests, you can always swing the other way.

Defining the Publishing Paths

Throughout the guide, I mention "traditional" and "independent" paths. But there are many different routes you can take for each, and it's not all about the Big New York publishers versus a one-person independent publishing business. For the sake of ease, when I mention these paths, they can include authors who publish in a myriad of different ways.

Traditional

Publishers:

- The "Big 5" Publishers–Simon & Schuster, Penguin Random House, HarperCollins, Hachette Book Group, and Macmillan.
- Smaller and independent presses–Tor, Scholastic, Kensington Publishing, Quirk Books, Algonquin Books, to name a few.

Independent

Publishing Routes:

- Solo self-publishing–An author publishing and distributing their own works.
- Solo independent press–An author creating a publishing imprint, only distributing their works.
- Hybrid press–A collaboration between an author and a publishing imprint. The author pays for some of, if not all, the costs of publishing (this is a vast range from editing to marketing) and the press distributes the book.
- Author co-ops/collectives–A collaboration where author-members share resources and time for editing, formatting, producing, and marketing books written by one or multiple authors.

The Pros and Cons

A perk of being a hybrid author is that you can choose what you want more often. Traditional authors have little choice in much of the publication process, and independent authors have a lot of expectations on their craft to perform and pay the bills.

In the next two sections, I'm breaking down the pros and cons of traditional and independent publishing. Please note, this is not a comprehensive list as my experience is limited to...well, my experience. You should form your opinion about either based on where you are now in your author journey. The learning process should never stop though, even if you are an author who wants to always be traditional or independent. Learning from either side can always benefit you, as both industries are in constant change.

Pros and Cons of Traditional Publishing

Prior to getting a book contract, the typical route is to find an agent and they will sell your books to editors at publishing houses. The querying process itself is a life lesson. Sure, you will come out with a champion who is in your corner to fight a lot of battles for you with publishing houses. But it takes kissing a lot of frogs before you find your princess.

The submission process can be time-consuming and disheartening when the rejections roll in. And they will. But this experience will toughen up the most sensitive writers, which is a plus, especially when you get your books published and have to deal with reviewer criticism. The pitching process is an important lesson to learn as well as you will repeat this process for every single book you publish, whether you are pitching to readers, publishing professionals, media, etc.

Book Production and Payments

Once you have a contract, you are paid a certain amount of money, an advance, for that book. If you have an agent, they receive the standard fifteen percent right out the gate for the lifetime of that book. The idea is to earn your publishing house that advance back so you can make royalties.

Now, you might make a nice advance and not feel you need to worry about earning it back, but when it comes to your next contract, they might offer less of an advance, or no contract at all if that previous book doesn't perform to their expectations.

If you are one of the lucky authors to earn out your advance, the royalties for your books are low, around or under 25% net receipts for digital formats such as eBook and audiobook, and around or under 15% for paperback or hardback. Some authors earn their advance back, most don't, so prepare yourself for making the exact amount of advance money, and no more.

In general, a traditional book will take eighteen months to two years from contract to publication. Those in digital-first or at smaller imprints may see a quicker timeline. The fastest I've experienced is three months between books, but that was with a digital-first imprint.

With traditional publishing, you have access to professional editors for free, which is a huge plus. The publishing house covers all production expenses, such as editing, distribution, and marketing, which is great as a low-risk cost investment toward your career.

When it comes to the production of the book, the author rarely has a say over the cover. In my experience, I've had some ability to request and get smaller tweaks, but not one of my covers has had major changes because of my dislike of it. And I've disliked a few (I still do). In addition to that, you have little say over formatting, or sub-right availability, such as paperback, audio, translations, and more.

Marketing

It's a misbelieve that all marketing falls to the publishing house. From my experience, the amount of marketing depends on how much the publisher has invested in your book. The more they invest, i.e., your advance, the more they will work to earn some or all of it back.

While publishers may put out advertisements such as banners or Times Square billboards, most of the time, it's behind-the-scenes actions that an author may never see, such as outreach to libraries and booksellers, sending review copies to sources such as Kirkus or Publishers

Weekly, and sending these advanced copies to their contacts. They may push your books to BookBub or other advertising services, but the transparency between publisher and author can be lacking.

Many traditional authors will use social media as their main advertising method, sometimes spending money on virtual or in-person tours. For years, I paid for blog tours, when they were popular and not so oversaturated as they are today. I've even paid freelance publicists in the past to help launch a book with me. The information learned from those experiences has allowed me to create more low-upfront cost tours with a growing list of influencers.

Discoverability

Being with a publishing house gives you access to their audience and clout. They have teams of people who understand their readers and know how to fit you into neat little boxes, i.e., the shelves at a bookstore. When it comes to bookstores, you will most likely get on shelves, but that is usually limited to your release month and in select stores.

With your connections with an agent (hopefully) and a publisher, you have been accepted through the "gates" and will have better access to them exercising sub-rights such as audiobooks, translation, and film rights. These are not always guaranteed, but you have better chances with a publisher who has a whole team dealing with these specific rights. This increases your discoverability and can be an immense asset, but be sure to push for them.

Also, you could work with your agent or a literary lawyer to revert some sub-rights after a period of time, but if you want more information about that, check out my other book, *Take Back Your Book: An Author's Guide to Rights*

Reversion and Publishing On Your Terms. I know authors who are successful with that and they are featured in this book.

With traditional publishers' reputations, you may earn more respect from your peers and readers because that's the path that is most known. Industry reviews will be easier to come by, depending on your genre, and you won't have to shell out the money for them. Examples are Kirkus, BookLife with Publisher's Weekly, and Library Journal.

Long-Term Success

This is harder to gauge with a traditional publisher. They are very data driven and sales numbers for your most recent releases are considered for the next contract. Authors who find long-term success usually write similar books because traditional publishing tends to move on the mindset of writing the same books over and over with slight variations. They thrive on readers coming back for what they love. This is not always the case, but tread lightly if you are a traditional author and want to write too far out of the box that was set for you.

I've learned so much through the process of traditionally publishing. I bypassed doing most of the work myself and had my hand held by knowledgeable professionals as we navigated publishing together. This has fast-tracked me to where I am now. I don't regret the path, and neither should you. Remember those catalogs? We're gaining the knowledge of the good, bad, and ugly, and forging our own paths using this information to guide us to a successful and lucrative career.

Pros and Cons of Independent Publishing

Book Production and Payments

As the publisher, you have control over all your rights and how the book is published. You choose your own editors, covers, formatting, marketing plans, promotions, and more. That upfront investment can be risky. The range for publishing a quality book can go from low hundreds to thousands, depending on what editors, designers, and marketing tactics you use. Technically, you can publish a book for free using the many direct platforms, but it's recommended that you spend money on professional cover designers and editors.

By doing it all yourself, you can receive higher royalties, around 70% per book, depending on the retailer, and even more if you directly sell from your website. Even though a publisher isn't taking a larger percentage, the platforms have operating costs, and some even take out delivery fees based on file size. But without proper marketing, there's the possibility of earning nothing from the book at all or struggling to make back what you spent.

The timeline for publishing a book is whatever you want it to be. You could rapidly release your books or choose to publish one a year. These choices are dictated by how quickly you can get through the writing and production process.

Marketing

Being an independent author gives you the flexibility to market and advertise your books however you want. You can take advantage of such strategies as permafree (which means that you make one of your books, usually the first of a series, permanently free and it's treated as a "loss leader" for your series to get readers hooked), or you can run free promotions, or 99-cent sales, the sky is the limit. Especially when traditional publishers end up taking over, i.e., flooding BookBub promotions and TikTok feeds. The ability to shift is key here.

Discoverability

A big issue for indie authors is visibility. There are so many books out there and the marketing landscapes are frequently changing. But with owning all the rights to your books and the ability to change pricing strategies, you have control to get the books into readers' hands. It may take creative ways of doing so, but ultimately, that control is a plus.

While it's difficult to gain access to certain aspects of the publishing industry, like film and translation rights, it's not impossible for indies. Literary agents can play an important role in exercising your sub-rights. Networking with other professionals in publishing and media could yield similar results, as more indie-friendly venues are cropping up.

Long-Term Success

By independently publishing, you can take more chances with your books. You can experiment with shorter or longer fiction, and create stories that are mashups of genres, giving your readers new experiences of entertainment and a broader range of fiction.

The independent publishing community is such a wealth of information, myth busting a lot of traditional publishing behind-the-scenes activities. Often, authors are open-minded about sharing their tactics and strategies and are willing to shout their successes to the masses in the hopes of building and maintaining the community as a whole.

Choosing the Hybrid Author Path

I may age myself here, but when I was a kid, I devoured *Choose Your Own Adventure*™ books. If you're not familiar, these books were like mazes of stories, with each big moment ending with a choice. You would pick one and jump to the page that would continue the story with that decision in mind.

This was incredibly fun for a creative and imaginative child. You had the opportunity to go down one path, and if that one didn't work out, you could go back and follow another, while having the knowledge of that previous one. If you read through enough, you could build up the world in your mind and know all the scenarios.

Being a hybrid author is a *Choose Your Own Adventure*™ path. You travel each route, filling your mind with all the options. Then, if you fall down a metaphorical well to your death (can you tell I write thrillers?), you can flip back to where you were before that and try again toward that path of ending the story with not a scratch on your body.

Now that you understand the pros and cons of traditional and independent publishing paths, I want to explain ways in which you can navigate both in succession to ramp up your reader base, sales, and backlist.

Publishing Speed

With traditional publishers it can take eighteen-months to two years, from inception through to publication, to get your book out there, and that's when you already have a contract. If you are just starting your writing career, it can take even longer since you would need to query agents first, but as a hybrid author, especially if you're a fast writer, you could independently publish in between traditional releases. Even better, the income you make from those independent books can fund your bills or the production process of more books between advances or royalty statements.

Money

Unless you have a massive book deal with tens of thousands of dollars' worth of an advance, independent authors tend to make more royalties on their books. You're not splitting royalties with a publishing house and agent fees. You're getting paid direct from the vendors such as Amazon and any platforms you choose to publish with. And if you are not enrolling your eBook in the KDP Select program, then you can even sell them direct from your website to get higher royalties.

On the other hand, if you have a good advance, or even better, are earning royalties, you can reinvest this money into your independent books. The cyclical nature of this may jumpstart your success as a hybrid author.

Genre Popularity

Traditional publishing leans toward releasing whatever genres make them the most money. This can be beneficial if you write in those specific genres, meaning you will most likely have future contracts. But when genres aren't widely popular anymore, traditional publishers seem to think they are "dead" and refuse to buy those books. But that's not always the case for readers. Voracious bibliophiles are constantly hungry for more books in their favorite genres. By independently publishing, you can explore those genres as much as you want while keeping some of the trendier ones in the traditional spaces.

For instance, the vampire trend was "out of favor" with traditional houses for a while after the *Twilight* era, but independently published authors continued writing vampires this whole time and have been making a lot of money from them.

Continuing a Series

Speaking of "death" in traditional publishing, many series are cut off too early. Each book has a finite amount of time to "perform" for a publisher before they get the axe. For instance, if you have a two-book deal for the start of a series, after you fulfilled that contract, the publisher will look at sales records before allowing you to continue writing for them. If the numbers aren't what they want them to be, then the series will stop, sometimes without giving the readers the satisfaction of a complete ending.

At that point, you've most likely spent years building up this readership with the intention of finishing the series with them. That disappointment is tough, especially when you have readers emailing you daily to continue the series, but by going hybrid you can keep that dream on track.

Depending on your option clause, you may be able to

revive this series and independently publish more books. Both Gail Carriger and Rachael Herron took this situation in different ways.

Gail Carriger has a wildly successful series that probably won't reach reversion anytime soon. Her love for the characters and their stories, along with a tight option clause, allow her to write in that series and independently publish those works, effectively satiating her fans, while also straddling the hybrid line.

Rachael Herron had a series that her publisher no longer wanted. Instead of leaving that series, she independently published the next books, and eventually was able to revert the earlier books and it is now completely independently published.

If you want to continue the series outside of your publisher, this comes with the possibility of a complicated issue. Depending on your contract, you would need to either get the permission of the publisher to continue the series on your own or you can ask for the rights to the series back when your reversion period is up.

Say your publisher still owns the rights to the published books and there is no issue with you continuing the series based on the contract (which you've checked with your agent, publisher, and/or lawyer, right?). Something to think about is the future of these books. There's the potential for the later books in the series to keep the traditional books in the series selling well. This may keep you future from reversion since those books will continue to make money. But, if you're continuing the series because you love it and you want to please your readers by continuing, then this is definitely a win.

But if you successfully reverted your series books, now you have full control over the published books and any books going forward. From there on, you can update the covers, formatting, everything to make the series more marketable as a whole.

Either way, the sky's the limit with the series and you can continue to write books, novellas, short stories, whatever you want to appease your readers and feed into that world that you love.

Another option is to publish a companion series. Again, that may bring readers to your trad-backlist, but now you have full control over all production of that series. Make sure to check your contract, and with your agent or a lawyer, to ensure that the characters, world, or likeness aren't owned by the publisher.

If you're coming from an independent space with your series, traditional publishers can take these books to new heights and allow you the opportunity to make more money from the series. Several examples of independent authors continuing series with traditional publishers include best-selling E. L. James with the Fifty Shades series, dark fantasy author, Scarlett St. Clair, and recent TikTok star, A. K. Mulford. James and St. Clair are with Bloom Books, Sourcebook's imprint for entrepreneurial women authors, and Harper Voyager acquired Mulford's books. More recently, the runaway success of Travis Baldree's 2021 NaNoWriMo project, *Legends & Lattes*, got him a massive deal with Tor and after republishing traditionally, it was an instant New York Times, Publisher's Weekly, USA Today, and Indie Bestseller. Now, it's being translated into nine additional languages.

Advertising and Promotion

This is a tricky one, because most publishing businesses, whether they are traditional or indie, rely on paid advertising. Though there are authors who focus more on different avenues. When it comes to the direct difference between marketing a traditional book or an independently published book, it comes down to control.

There is a barrier when it comes to advertising books you don't own the rights to. When I dabbled with Facebook ads for my traditional books, I came up with several roadblocks in determining their effectiveness. Royalty reports from publishers can come two months to a year in the rears, depending on your contract. Also, those reports didn't break down the sales by platform or by week. Sure, I tracked ranking on Amazon, but with advertising, you need more data.

When it comes to promotions, with my traditional publishers, I didn't have to spend much. They would submit and pay for any BookBub deals, which was great. But I had no idea when those promotions were coming until they were set on the calendar. While I know things are going on behind the scenes with my traditional books, as a mid-list author without a huge promotional backing, I wish there was more transparency. I'm incredibly grateful for those opportunities because they don't come for free, even for the publisher. But in the vein of sharing, as I've experienced so much more with the indie community, I believe that if traditional publishers worked with their authors more collaboratively, then we could all succeed together.

As I've moved into independent publishing, I've learned so much when it comes to promotions. I've learned that authors continuously apply for BookBub promotions, and once they get rejected, they try again. Then there are the free options for promotion, involving other authors, such as book and newsletter swaps, using that community aspect to help promote their books. Or, if you have a series, that the permafree tactic is quite successful. When you control all aspects of your books, you have more flexibility with advertising and promotion, and can take risks that pay off well.

Publishing Experiments

Many traditional authors struggle with the lack of control over their books or are unaware of all the possibilities that publishing has to offer. Without the control, sometimes you are leaving money on the table.

As the independent publishing possibilities expand every year, indie authors are jumping on strategies to get more of their books into readers' hands.

For instance, direct sales have been a huge conversation for a while. When it comes to social and distribution platforms, nothing is infallible. Any website that you don't own can and will break. What happens when Facebook goes down and all your advertising money no longer works for you? Or if the algorithm isn't favoring you on Amazon or social media platforms?

Many indie authors are holding tight to what they control, and that is their books. If you want to make this an actual career, you should have as much control as possible to squeeze every penny from each sale. When indie publishing inherently offers more money per sale, why not take more?

A lot of indie authors are moving to a point where their books are available directly from them. Katie Cross is an example of a success story as she is treating her author business more like a retailer. She is still on the major eBook platforms but has incredible deals and promotions on her books to divert readers to her website instead of Amazon. If you are interested in one model of direct sales as an author, she is one that I constantly look toward for advice.

If you are a traditional author, direct sales are still

available to you. You will have to purchase physical books from your publisher at a discount to have them in stock for online sales or book events.

Direct sales are only an example. There are authors right now making life-changing money on Kickstarter and other crowdfunding platforms, and I'm sure there are more experimental ways to come.

Frontlist versus Backlist

Traditional publishing tends to focus on their frontlists. There is such a huge marketing push toward these books, and if you are one of them, then you are set up very well. Once the season is over, they move right along, taking their marketing and advertising money to upcoming books. That might include yours, depending on how the book performed.

This was an unknown problem for me early in my career. After *The Life After* series was published, I wanted to find more readers for it, but I was encouraged to move onto the next book. So I stayed the course on the publishing treadmill, unable to look back at the other books in my catalog.

It wasn't until I made more contacts with indie authors that I realized the shift. A lot of indie authors focus on their backlist and are constantly promoting previous books they've written.

To me, this is a no-brainer. If you've spent time writing, publishing, and marketing your book, why just forget about it after a few months? This is something that astonishes me about traditional publishing. Why not make that book work for you in the way that you've worked for it?

Using a hybrid method, you can also do that big launch push, even better if you're able to use a traditional book to gain readership but forget about your backlist. Take time to plan promotions, add different formats, box sets, special editions, and more to your backlist. For books with your publisher, work with them to bundle your series, or push for an audiobook, or ask to run a sale with them, among many other options.

Pros and Cons of a Hybrid Path

Book Production and Payments

As a hybrid author, you can write all the books of your heart and find the audience for them. But that comes at a cost of time and money.

With independent publishing, you wear all the hats of production and marketing. This is a huge time and cost investment. So, at what point are you able to tackle traditional projects? Even though you have a publishing partner with your traditional books, how do you balance the independent ones when you're on traditional deadlines?

This can be frustrating for those who have families, full-time jobs, or other situations where their time isn't always theirs. Some authors appreciate the ability to write books and send them off to their editors and let the publishing house do all the work, which can be an advantage for a hybrid author, giving you a little more time to work on your independent books.

It takes a realistic view of your finances and time. Intelligently reinvesting from traditional advances and independent royalties can supplement the production and marketing costs of your books.

On the other hand, when it comes to payments, you have the possibility of hitting all the pros of both publishing avenues. If you're consistently getting contracts with your traditional books, that money is guaranteed, but with creative budgeting, you can use this seed money to filter into your independent books, which will give you a significant amount more in royalties.

Marketing

Hybrid authors have an advantage when it comes to marketing their books due to the unique insights and skills they possess from both traditional and independent publishing experiences. Whether it's through utilizing existing platforms, engaging with audiences directly on social media, or experimenting with new marketing techniques, hybrid authors can effectively promote their books and reach a wider audience. This gives them a competitive edge in the publishing landscape, as well as the ability to grow their brand and cultivate long-term success. Using your publisher as clout to say, for example, "I was a best-selling author with Simon and Schuster" or listing trade reviews for your traditional books is always a plus when it comes to marketing. You can also use any trade reviews from your books to elevate your indie-published ones as well.

To create a book marketing campaign, hybrid authors should focus on understanding their target audience and identifying the best strategies to reach them. This may include utilizing existing platforms, such as social media or email marketing, creating targeted ads, or partnering with other authors and influencers in the industry. Furthermore, you can continuously experiment with new tactics and strategies to stay ahead of the competition and keep your marketing efforts fresh and engaging. By being strategic and data-driven in your approach, you can achieve significant success in promoting your books and building your brand as an author.

Additionally, hybrid authors may neglect actively monitoring and analyzing the performance of their marketing efforts by looking at sales data on their distributor's platforms, which can lead to missed opportunities or ineffective strategies. For success in book marketing, you must continuously be aware of emerging trends and best practices in the industry, such as subscribing to Publishers Marketplace, staying active within the author community, and adapt your approach accordingly. You can do this by joining author groups and staying on top of industry trends in both the independent publishing and traditional publishing spaces. By doing so, you can avoid common mistakes and maximize the success of their book marketing campaigns.

Being a hybrid author can be beneficial when you combine the two paths. Your experience with your audience, coupled with the backing of a traditional publisher gives you the ability to reach more readers and potentially increase the visibility and popularity of your books. Independent marketing methods, on the other hand, can be more targeted and personalized, allowing the author to connect with their audience on a deeper level. Combining these approaches gives you the ability to leverage the strengths of each approaches.

By combining the two approaches, a hybrid author can leverage the strengths of both methods to create a more effective marketing campaign. This may also appeal to authors who prefer to have more control over their promotional activities.

Discoverability

One major advantage of being a hybrid author is that

this path offers greater exposure and visibility for your work. Since hybrid authors can reach both traditional and independently published audiences, they can potentially attract more readers than authors who only publish through one channel. This can help build your brand and increase your sales over time, as you're able to publish more books than someone who is pursuing only one of the paths.

Additionally, creating your own website or blog that is linked to all your publishers and distributors ensures that you can control the narrative around your brand, allowing potential readers to learn more about you and become interested in your books.

If you are a hybrid author looking to improve your discoverability, there are several things that you can do to help increase your reach and attract more readers. First, make sure that your work is available in multiple formats so it can be easily accessible on all platforms. Likewise, ensure that all your publishers and distributors have accurate information about you that they can share with potential readers–including links to any personal social media accounts or websites that you may have. Finally, focus on building a positive brand reputation by creating high-quality content, developing healthy relationships with your readers and building a backlist.

One of the biggest downsides of discoverability for hybrid authors is that it can be difficult to get your work in front of readers. Many platforms and services are highly focused on specific genres or categories, making it hard to reach audiences outside of these confines. Additionally, without a large following or established platform, it can be very challenging for authors to gain attention for their work.

Another downside of discoverability for hybrid authors

is that there can be a lot of competition. With so many authors vying for readers' attention, it's tough to stand out from the crowd and make your voice heard. This can make promoting yourself particularly challenging, especially if you do not have any prior experience with marketing or self-promotion.

There are many strategies and techniques that hybrid authors can use to improve their discoverability. By focusing on building a strong online presence and networking with other writers and readers, it is possible to increase your reach and boost your profile. Ultimately, the key to success as a hybrid author is finding new and innovative ways to get your work in front of audiences, no matter what platform or service you choose.

An alternative way to increase discoverability is to push for as many sub-rights as you can. Understanding where most of your audience is can be key to success. Independent authors can get an agent to sell audio, film, and translation rights, or take advantage of these avenues with their traditional books. The more formats you have, the more opportunities you have for audience growth and increased income.

Long-Term Success

While being a hybrid author can certainly be a pathway to long-term success, there are also some potential downsides. One major challenge is the management and balance of multiple publication channels simultaneously. This can be both time consuming and difficult, especially if you do not have a dedicated marketing or PR team to help with the process.

Despite these challenges, there are many benefits for long-term success, including increased exposure, greater control over marketing and promotion, and the ability to reach a wider range of readers. Ultimately, hybrid authors who put in the time, effort, and dedication to succeed will be able to reap the benefits of this dynamic publishing model for many years to come.

Pitfalls

I conducted a survey with several hybrid authors who had so many great gems of information about their personal pitfalls of being hybrid.

Katie MacAlister and I agree that on the traditional side, some editors aren't pushing for marketing as much as they used to, unfortunately. A pitfall of indie publishing is doing all the work, paying for that work, and the time and cost commitment of marketing.

Golden Angel feels a big pitfall is giving control over to someone else. While it can be freeing to hand off a book to an agent and wait for the contract, when it inevitably comes, you have no control over much after that, including the cover, sales data, and marketing efforts. It also takes a lot more time to get a book on the shelf as a traditional than indie. She feels she couldn't be a full-time author without her indie income.

Kat Cantrell feels the same way that a lot of hybrid authors do in that we don't have enough time to write all the books we want to.

Sharon Wray agrees that independent publishing is a lot of work, especially when you are just starting off and putting a lot of money out up front when you're only getting paid from a traditional publisher twice a year. As I've mentioned, contracts can vary. For the first eight books that I published, I still only see royalties once a quarter, whereas my most recent contract sends statements out monthly.

Sara Rosett mentioned a common pitfall in that if you are coming into hybrid author status as an indie, you might find it frustrating to have little control over much when it comes to your traditional books. Even with no control, the expectations from your publisher are that you need to take part in promotions, yet you're not given the data on those efforts, or at least not in the detail necessary to make significant tweaks.

Claire Wilder has trouble with compartmentalizing the work for both her indie and traditional books. She, like a lot of authors, struggle to do both at the same time, so in the end, one of the books or series suffers for it.

Myth Busting

Throughout the years, there has been such a divide between traditional publishing and independent publishing authors. I believe the traditional system and author expectations perpetuates this. But independent publishing is getting closer to their traditional counterparts as the technology advances for indie authors, but the stigma remains, depending on who you speak to.

I started writing about books in a blog years before I considered publishing, so I have a perspective as a reader, reviewer, and author. Even in the reading community, the divide between traditional and indie-published books was a hard line that not a lot of people crossed.

For me, I found some of my favorite books of all time through indie authors. This was the start to keeping an open mind about the different publishing paths and placing value in them. Because authors wouldn't be doing either if there wasn't the ability to make money and a living off their works.

Many of the myths that come with being a hybrid author are that one of your "sides" is better or different than the other, so much so that there needs to be sides at all!

As I've already outlined, there are pros and cons of going solely traditional or independent. Learning the most you can about both these processes will only make your decisions have more weight, but also you can start to bend the stigma of "one or the other" by understanding on a deeper level which books you can take to either path.

One of the most common myths surrounding hybrid authors is that they don't need to market their books at all. This idea stems from the belief that hybrid authors have a built-in audience through their other products, such as eBooks or courses, and therefore don't need to spend time or resources on marketing their books. This is simply not true. Regardless of your publishing status or whether you have an existing audience, hybrid authors still need to build a marketing strategy and actively promote their books.

To overcome this myth, hybrid authors can focus on building strategic partnerships with other authors and influencers in their niche. Whether it's cross-promoting books, guest posting on influential blogs, or using paid advertising opportunities, hybrid authors can leverage these relationships to get discovered by more readers and grow their author career.

Some believe that hybrid authors don't take their craft seriously, or that they simply write for money rather than passion. However, nothing could be further from the truth.

Hybrid authors are just as dedicated to their craft as any other author. They produce high-quality work on a consistent basis and spend countless hours honing their skills and improving their writing techniques. In addition, these authors value quality over quantity, focusing on creating well-written stories rather than rushing to meet arbitrary word count goals set by traditional publishers.

The survey that I conducted with some authors offered some examples of myths that they've heard of surrounding hybrid authors.

An interesting myth that I learned from Golden Angel is that people assume that your big sellers and income earners come from your traditional books, and indie books are more for passion projects. This is simply not true. Golden focuses on marketing and promoting the books she controls and earns higher royalties than her traditional books.

On the other side, is author Kat Cantrell who states that she makes very good money on her traditional contracts, and indie books aren't the only place to make that full-time income.

While I believe that hybrid is the best of both worlds, Sara Rosett challenges that mindset with her own twist, in that being hybrid isn't always that way, as it depends on many things like your situation, your personality, and your definition of success. Which I think is a great point, as nothing in this business comes from throwing spaghetti at the wall. Intention, dedication, and creativity all play a part in publishing, no matter if you're indie, traditional, or hybrid.

Case Study: Sacha Black

Sacha Black is a bestselling fantasy fiction writer with a growing list of nonfiction writing craft books for writers including *The Anatomy of Prose: 12 Steps to Sensational Sentences* and *13 Steps to Evil: How to Craft Superbad Villains*.

Initial Path to Publication

She started her author journey as an independent author. Working in the corporate world for many years deterred her from allowing anyone, especially another corporate company, to control the rights to her books.

Early in her writing career, finishing her first book gave her the idea that she could be a writer and she wanted to know all the things. As a lifelong learner, she researched everything she could about publishing, most notably some giants in the independent publishing arena, such as Joanna Penn, the Alliance of Independent Authors (ALLi), Bryan Cohen, et al. The business and financial aspects of independent publishing spoke to her more than the possibility of another company controlling the rights to her art. During our chat, the word that jumped out at me the most was her feeling "vulnerable". She didn't want someone else to make the decisions for her when it came to her income or her books, as her day job already had seized control over most of her life.

In 2017, Sacha found success in publishing her first non-fiction book for writers, *13 Steps to Evil: How to Craft Superbad Villains*. This book found her on a successful stream of AMS (Amazon Marketing Services) advertising and on podcasts where she promoted her book to her ideal audience. Since then, she's published a four-book fantasy series and more non-fiction books for writers.

Becoming Hybrid

Her path to becoming a hybrid author stemmed from an interesting email in her inbox. A Korean publisher reached out to obtain the translation rights for all her current non-fiction titles.

From this conversation, we delved into how selling subrights can help authors use their intellectual property to further their reader base regarding opportunities that they couldn't do themselves or don't have the capacity to do. For Sacha, hiring a translator, editor, and being able to market to a Korean readership was something she felt she wasn't capable of doing on her own. This opportunity made business sense for her as she now is linked with a professional who can handle the translations and has the capacity to do so. Both sides "win" in this scenario.She reached out to an agent associated with the Alliance of Independent Authors (ALLi). They were able to broker a deal with the publisher that gave Sacha much more than the initial contract.

Income Diversification

In terms of being hybrid, Sacha's method of diversification heavily weighs on being selective in selling subrights. She's also considering going traditional with a new genre of books as, currently, the big traditional book publishers have most of the books in this genre under their control. But this move will be strategic, and the willingness to give up full rights weighed against not. There are different factors involved in her decision, such as whether she's writing a standalone book or a series, if she wants to apply for awards or a film deal—which is notoriously difficult for indie authors (but never impossible!).

Balancing Lists

One of the surprising bits of being a hybrid author was experiencing the freedom of this traditional deal with the Korean publisher. She hasn't had much to do other than a few emails back and forth with her agent, which she feels is a blessing and a curse. Indie's rarely give up control, but it can feel freeing after lifting the heavy load on your own!

Another interesting part of our conversation was inclusivity when it came to marketing. Sacha wasn't sure how she could market these translated books, but the indie spirit of including links on her website and social media, etc., and showing her support of those books and her publisher, can only help sales.

This may involve including links to other books or products on your website or social media or reaching out to publishers to collaborate on marketing efforts. Ultimately, by engaging with readers and building connections across different parts of the publishing industry, you can promote your hybrid author status to reach new audiences and build long-term success.

Throughout the process of becoming a hybrid author, Sacha found it empowering to have control over her books, while choosing which rights to give up and how those contracts were structured.

One key factor to consider when marketing as a hybrid author is the role that control plays in your decision-making process. While it may feel empowering to have full control over your books, it can also be difficult to manage all aspects of book production and promotion alone. To navigate this challenge, it is important to seek out the support of agents and other experts who can help you make informed decisions and maximize the benefits of your hybrid author status.

Actionable Steps

The piece of advice that she has for other authors who are given a contract is placing a period of pause on the decision to sign. This is incredibly important because we, as creatives, can get so much validation and excitement when someone wants our books or sub-rights for said books, that a lot of authors (myself included when I was a wee naive author) will sign right away without even considering the future options. Traditional publishers are getting smarter and writing tighter clauses, keeping their interests in mind for the investment they are putting in your book, like cover design, editing, and marketing dollars. It's so important to have an agent, and Sacha was incredibly smart to seek out that help prior to negotiations and got more money and a better deal for her books out of it.

Going Hybrid

Now that we're through the basics of hybrid publishing, here's where the work starts. As you've considered your own path, let's talk about some of the important logistics of the process of going from one status to the other.

From Traditionally Published Author to Hybrid Author

As I started on this route, I found it fitting to begin here. But even if you are starting out as an independent author, I would suggest reading through all the sections to get the full breadth of information.

If you began on this path, there are several directions you can take with your books. As a traditional author, you have the unique hurdle of option clauses and rights reversion.

Contract Clauses

With contracts, there are a lot of limiting clauses, especially your option clause. This clause offers the publisher first refusal of your next book. For example, an option clause might read:

> *The Author agrees to give the Publishers the first option to consider for publication the Author's next work of a similar nature ('Next Work') subject to the same terms as set out in this Agreement unless mutually agreed otherwise. Within 90*

*days of receipt of a reasonably detailed synopsis and the first
three chapters of the Next Work, the Publishers shall inform
the Author whether they wish to publish it.*

This is a point of contention with a lot of authors and
literary agents and it's imperative that you make it as tight
as possible so that you aren't limited to what you can
publish in the future. What does that mean? Say you write
women's fiction, and you only want to publish those books
traditionally, make sure the language in the option clause
states that. Another tip is to set limits on how long the
publisher will have to make their decision on whether they
want to publish your next work. A literary lawyer or agent
will be able to help you with this as they are the experts,
but definitely look at this section, and all the others in your
contract. This is especially important if you are wanting to
independently publish.

Looking at the example, the first thing I would high-
light is defining that Next Work. As I mentioned above, if
you write women's fiction, I urge a clarifying line in that
text to read something like:

*The Author agrees to give the Publishers the first option to
consider for publication the Author's next women's fiction
novel ('Next Work').*

Or an even tighter example would be:

*The Author agrees to give the Publishers the first option to
consider for publication the Author's next women's fiction
novel set in the same fiction universe as this book ('Next
Work').*

Within the timeline, you can ask to make a quicker

turnaround than the 90 days for the synopsis and chapters. I would whittle that down to as quick as they would agree to, because imagine waiting 90 days for an answer on whether you can move forward on a project or not.

Another way that you can become a hybrid author using the books in your backlist is through rights reversion. The right to revert on the book is another contractual clause which gives you the opportunity to, in essence, take back your book from the publisher. Usually there are terms involved, for example:

> *If three years after publication, your royalty statements bring in less than $100 per quarter, then you have the right to revert.*

Like option clauses, these reversion clauses differ widely. For instance, two books that I currently have with a publisher won't revert until two years after three books I have in a later contract.

I always recommend making sure you are educated on all the clauses and asking your agent for help is usually the first step. If you don't have an agent, hire a literary lawyer to help. This investment will pay-off significantly during your career. Also, there are many writer organizations out there who offer services like this, such as the Alliance of Independent Authors (ALLi) and The Authors Guild, to name a few. Research and make sure that you are well versed and comfortable with the language before signing any contract.

Going Indie

If you can overcome these clauses and you are either writing a new book or publishing a reverted book, going indie might be a bit of a shock. At least it was for me. Up until this point, you've only had to worry about writing and editing the book, and possibly doing some launch tasks. After that, it's usually advised for authors to start working on the next book.

I equate traditional publishing to a treadmill. Once you hop on, usually you move at a steady pace. You start off walking (i.e., writing and editing), you add a bit of an incline once you get your cover and a release date, then you kick up the speed toward launch. By then, you might be a sweaty mess and ready to jump off, but your editor slows the speed down and you work on the next book together. Then you rinse and repeat.

Moving toward independent publishing, I find the correlation more like an elliptical machine. Using your own strength, you overcome the resistance that you set for yourself. You can begin with no resistance and push through all the publication tasks, and as you become more proficient with that setting and try something new, you add a little more resistance until you overcome that and push harder.

While both exercises are perfectly acceptable, they tend to strengthen different parts of your body to create a more balanced physique, or in this case, career. Neither is easy per se, but becoming informed in different aspects of publishing, you're able to control more of your career than you thought.

Trying to independently publish gives you the opportunity to understand what goes on behind the mystery veil of traditional publishing. Those nuances of summary writing, applying for advertising, formatting, proofreading, and distribution, to name a few, will only make you appreciate the work done to get a book on shelves. It may even offer you the ability to understand what some of these aspects mean for your time and budget and help decide whether staying traditional is better for you. But you wouldn't know for sure until you peek over the fence of independent publishing.

Coming to independent publishing from a traditional space, there is much to learn about the process. It's no longer just writing and editing. You become writer, publisher, and marketer. While there is more freedom in choosing advertising and marketing methods and having access to updating your books in the future, there is a lot of work to be done. I would suggest researching as much as possible before diving in.

There are a lot of free or inexpensive opportunities out there. Listening to podcasts or watching YouTube channels on how to publish, such as The Creative Penn, or joining writer groups. I've found many on Facebook such as the Alliance of Independent Authors, Wide for the Win, and 20 Books to 50k ™. Then there are courses. If you are investing in a course, make sure it's the right one for you as some don't offer as much as others, but still cost the same or more than the reputable ones. One of my favorite courses that is both evergreen and constantly growing is Publish and Thrive, created by Sarra Cannon. These are just a few of many out there, and don't feel the need to know everything up front.

My advice would be to take it one book at a time. Whether you're starting off like I did with a reverted book or a new one, complete the writing and editing process first. Then work with a cover designer, learn about formatting or hire out for it, understand how each distributor works or start off with Amazon KDP Select before going wide. Once the book is out, learn new marketing methods one at a time before moving onto the next. By chunking the tasks into smaller ones, you may appreciate the process more without feeling overwhelmed.

I also suggest creating a network of other independent authors who are at your level and a little ahead of you. This way, you can learn while also experiencing the highs and lows together. The unique part of independent publishing is that even though it seems like a competition, there are enough readers of books to go around, so working with others will only benefit you.

As a traditionally published author, you may be looking for ways to write similar books and indie-publish them while still under contract with your publisher. One strategy that hybrid authors often use is to write and publish similar books within the same genre or niche in order to reach a wider audience and tap into existing reader bases. By leveraging your existing publishing relationships and platforms, you can continue to grow and expand your author career by reaching new readers through multiple channels. Whether this involves experimenting with different writing styles or utilizing marketing strategies like promotions or giveaways, there are many tools available for hybrid authors to promote their work and build their brand in the publishing world.

Case Study: Rachael Herron

Rachael Herron is the internationally best-selling author of more than two dozen books, including thrillers (under R. H. Herron), mainstream fiction, feminist romance, memoir, and nonfiction about writing.

Initial Path to Publication

In 2006, there weren't a lot of widely available options yet for indie publishing, so when she finished her book, she got an agent and sold it to a publisher in 2008 in a three-book deal. Those books came out in 2010, 2011, 2012. Then she received another contract from HarperCollins Publishers after that. So, at that point, she was firmly in the traditional publishing space, publishing one book a year.

Rachael strongly encourages authors who want to be traditional to absolutely pursue that route if it's good for them.

Becoming Hybrid

It wasn't until a lunch with a fellow author, Bella Andre, that the conversation of rights reversion came up. Andre had put her reverted books online and was making a significant amount of money from them. But even with that evidence of success, Rachael found herself holding back a little, since at that time, there was still a negative stigma surrounding independent publishing.

In one of her series, the books themselves became hybrid. HarperCollins didn't want books four and five, but Penguin Australia did. As Rachael and her agent had kept world rights with that contract, Rachael was able to publish those books herself, outside of Australia, and did the same with several others.

I find that process interesting, because over the years, I've heard of agents and authors trying to keep as many rights as possible, especially when it comes to world rights. But I'd never heard of books themselves going hybrid until speaking with Rachael. This is a point to consider, depending on the size of your deal and which publisher you sign with.

After that, Rachael seemed to get a taste for independent publishing, stemming from the route that many starting traditional authors do, with rights reversion. As her books reverted to her, she was able to publish them on their own, including a 10-year anniversary edition and audiobook of her memoir, *A Life in Stitches*. Eventually, she got the first three books back from that original series, giving her full control of all five books.

When it comes to choosing which books to be traditional and indie-published, Rachael bases her decision per book. At the time of our conversation, she mentioned wanting to have her agent sell her thrillers but wanted to hold back on her recent memoir that she has already worked with an editor on, with the initial intent to indie-publish.

The part that interested me most was the conversation she had with her agent. Rachael offered the book to her agent for a limited amount of time to pitch to publishers for Big Money, and nothing less. Big Money is six-figures for Rachael. If she's going to give up the rights to a publisher, then she wants to ensure that the Big Money gets the attention it deserves. Frequently, when we're talking about the traditionally published authors with marketing budgets, it's really the ones that publishers have invested in who receive those bigger budgets, with billboards in Times Square or massive tours and campaigns. If publishers aren't invested in recouping their money, those marketing budgets plummet, and for some, are non-existent outside of a few tweets or Instagram posts.

Income Diversification

One benefit of being a hybrid author that sticks with Rachael (and me now that I know about it!) is that hybrid authors make more money than a solely traditional or a solely independent author. The many ways that you can strategically position your books at any point in your author career allows creativity to extend outside of your stories. Becoming a champion and marketer for your books on either publishing path allows a broader view of the trajectory of your career and all the possibilities within it.

Balancing Lists

As an author with ADHD, Rachael often finds herself motivated and inspired to work on different aspects of her indie books and loves that she can follow where her brain and interest go. Also, having a mix of the control and lack of control is good for her as well.

I wholeheartedly agree with this. As an ADHD-suspecting adult, I could never put into words why I went off and published so many genres, a mistake that I don't necessarily regret, but have been course-correcting so that I can find my audience and they can find my books. Also, as I've been publishing solely indie for a bit now, the control is great, but when I've had conversations with my publisher about my backlist (mostly when I'm asking for reversion), having them deal with those books is equally calming for my brain.

When it comes to "mistakes", Rachael feels that there are none, only a grand science experiment in publishing. While she used to lose sleep over little errors, she doesn't anymore. And with more control over her books, the ability to course-correct is much easier than with the traditional books.

I used to be like that with my traditional books. In the first iteration of my debut, there was a continuity error that went out with the book, and I was devastated. I wrote to my editor, begging them to fix it. I lost days of writing, agonizing over it. In the end, my request went ignored, as a lot of them did, but I also know that so many books go out with errors. As an indie author, I'm meticulous about my decisions, but also, with all that control, there's a freedom that comes from it. If I do make a mistake, I know I can change it. If I want to change the covers five years down the line, I don't need to ask for permission. Mistakes can get made, but with that greater control, comes more relief than grief.

Actionable Steps

Play and experiment with your books and remember to have fun. This is often lost in the daily grind of writing and publishing, and often when she's feeling like it's all a slog, she changes her mind set to "how can I make this fun" or shifting to another aspect of publishing that is more engaging at that moment.

For me, when I'm stuck, I usually feel the brakes from my brain telling me to stop. This is something I've noticed over the years, and I listen. I will definitely adopt a more "fun" attitude toward these moments, thanks to Rachael.

From Independently Published Author to Hybrid Author

There are several ways you can gain that hybrid author status from independent publishing first. You could have started off independent publishing and been a runaway success when an editor or agent found you and brought you into the fold. Or you might have had a steady career in independent publishing but want to widen your audience and distribution. You could be interested in keeping your IP or intellectual property, i.e., your book, but you want to sell sub-rights such as audio or foreign translations. Or you may want to take your career in a new direction with a new genre or target age.

Engaging with Publishers

You could go the typical route by writing a new book and querying agents and editors. You could also reach out to agents or editors, citing your backlist and royalty reports. Most of the time, if you are shopping a book that's already been published, you will find the most success if you are just that, a success. Or if you want to pitch a new series to be traditionally published, you may have to show receipts that you have been successful with other books in the past. That way, agents and editors see that you already have a built-in audience for you and them to sell to. Getting an audience for a new author is half the battle for publishers, so coming into the conversation with readers already looking for your next book puts you ahead from the jump.

If you are an author who has published several books and no one has bought them, it's going to be a little more difficult to sell yourself to agents and editors without offering a new premise and book. While there is nothing wrong with starting here, I would recommend taking the path of writing a new book and querying agents with it. Or you can always use a pen name.

If you are interested in keeping your intellectual property (usually at least eBook and print) but want to diversify and you either don't have the time or energy to put toward researching and contacting freelancers to put out audiobooks and other sub-rights, you can approach publishers. Sometimes, like in Helen Scheuerer's case study, publishers approached her. You can reach out to them yourself as well. Again, you will probably have to "prove" yourself to make it worthwhile to the publisher. This usually comes with your ability to show that you have an audience ready to buy these other versions of your book or expanding your audience.

If you'd like to try traditional publishing outside of the books and genre you've already published, that is a valid path as well. I see many authors use pen names when they move out of their genre, and how you want to separate your brands is up to you, but depending how close the genres are, you may be able to get by with tweaking your first or last name or adding initials to the author's name to distinguish the types of books you write, if you want to at all.

Previously, indie authors had an advantage coming from this strategy. This is under the assumption that you've done a lot of the book production and administrative work yourself, such as hiring designers and editors, along with possibly formatting the book yourself, and putting the book on distributor websites. At this point, you have the knowledge of the intricacies of creating a book-shaped thing. Traditional publishing can bring an author to the top of the charts, but there are nuances to becoming one of those authors, and you must give a lot to get a lot in return. By giving, I mean percentages of royalties and control. As I mentioned, you have an advantage here because you've seen what you can do for your books in the creation of them, marketing, and return on investment, or ROI. You've already learned so much with marketing to your readers that you can turn those skills into marketing yourself to agents and publishers. You can use praise quotes or relationships with authors, booksellers, or librarians to show how much of an asset you will be to a traditional house.

Case Study: Helen Scheuerer

Helen Scheuerer is the author of the bestselling young adult fantasy series, *The Oremere Chronicles*. She studied creative writing at university and has a Master's of Publishing. Her most recent nonfiction title is a fantastic actionable read titled, *How to Write a Successful Series*.

Initial Path to Publication

Helen started her career, as most do with creative writing at university, with pursuing a deal for a literary novel. After she secured a deal with a small press, she worked for almost two years with an editor on structural edits.

During that time, she fell out of love with the process and realized that she wasn't writing what she was interested in reading. So, between edits, she wrote a fantasy novel for herself, and decided to publish it on her own.

A blessing in disguise came her way when the small press closed and reverted all rights to the literary fiction novel back to her. Her intent, now, was to publish the fantasy books that she'd been writing.

Throughout the time that her literary novel was with the publisher and writing the fantasy novel, Helen wrote about her process on her blog. In doing so, she'd caught the attention of an editor at one of the big New York publishers. To her, this felt like another test, as when she had a conversation with the editor, they said it would take almost two months to have a final decision on if she would get a contract. In the end, Helen wanted to publish sooner than that and didn't want to pause the progression of her book for two months with the possibility of not getting a contract at all. This was the final push for her to decide to indie-publish first.

Becoming Hybrid

The first book in the series, *Heart of Mist*, gained enough recognition that Helen was approached by two different audiobook publishers for those rights.

I find this part interesting because Helen didn't, at the time, want to narrate or produce her own audiobooks in that series. These types of decisions for indies are not taken lightly. Those who are independent publishing only have enough hours in the day to be the author and publisher, so, she had her agent handle the deal and Audible ended up winning the audiobook rights for *The Oremere Chronicles*.

Helen also took a bit of control with her contract and had it written in there that she wanted certain specifications on the narrator. She wanted a female, British voice to narrate the novels as her main character and target audience were female. She was sent samples and had approval over the voice, which was important to her. Many traditional authors don't get this courtesy, which is another part of a contract to investigate.

As Helen is firmly invested in independent publishing of her books, her agent handles all the audiobook sub-rights only. Even as she's gone off to publish a non-fiction book, *How to Write a Successful Series* she still intends only to give sub-rights to her agent.

A frustration that she and I shared was the lack of communication surrounding publishers and marketing. We have both asked our respective publishers to offer what their plan is so that we can help elevate a book (or in Helen's case, her audiobooks) and were either met with no answer or vague ones. She dives into this a bit deeper when talking about targeted marketing. She looks at comparative titles ("comp titles") and finds readers who like those books and focuses on them. Whereas publishers tend to cast a wider net. That isn't always the case, but from Helen's perspective and mine, it certainly feels that way.

Income Diversification

When we talk about the main benefits of being a hybrid author, Helen makes an excellent point in that without taking these traditional deals, there most likely wouldn't be these products out there and she might not have reached those specific audiobook listeners on her own.

With that diversification of income, it came to be a blessing in disguise, as she was one of those unfortunate authors caught up in Amazon's account lockdown situation.

This seems to happen frequently to independent authors who are enrolled in the KDP Select program. Often, these authors are cited a list of triggers such as

Amazon needing proof that these authors own the copyright for the materials (which is quite difficult to prove when you are an indie), or by using certain phrases or words in your title. The copyright issue hits reverted titles quite often as Amazon may notice that a similar or even the same book was published before.

Helen has her books enrolled in the KDP Select program so when her account was shut down, her main source of income, which pays her living expenses, halted. Fortunately, her audiobooks weren't affected. It's a scary situation for a lot of authors and by diversifying her income with sub-right deals and physical copies, she was able to hold on with those avenues until Amazon reinstated her account.

Balancing Lists

As a full-time author, Helen is extremely busy with creating new content for her front list, but what about her ever-growing backlist? Every quarter, Helen strategically runs a sale and runs giveaways to promote her lead magnets, the shorter stories that lead into either of the series. She's constantly advertising the first books in the series to lead readers to read through the rest. She also has her catalog listed in her newsletter that she sends out twice a month for her more dedicated fans. As Helen is really invested in the series mindset, she finds an unfinished series a bit of a hurdle to overcome and has plans to promote in different ways when her future series is complete for readers.

During the time it takes for her to get the series out, she's still giving her readers teasers in the way of short stories and novellas through the newsletter. Even though that can be difficult to keep up with as an indie, especially one that's releasing massive fantasy novels once or twice a year, it's one of the important things to keep your readers aware of your progress with a series and tease them into reading the next books you're producing.

Helen struggles with the idea of having the faith that her publishers are doing their best to promote her books, at least looking through the lens of how she would. Much of the onus is on her to ask for their campaigns.

A common theme throughout the conversation is taking as much control over the process as you can. Knowing that you can fight for what you want in a contract and standing up for yourself, and for your books, is a mindset that all authors should possess if you want to make this career yours.

I admire Helen's mindset when it comes to publishing. It's a skill that, when honed, can be such an important part of a creative business. By looking at books through the lens of a product, you can use your creativity in another way. Helen looked at the top selling books in her catalogue and utilized a gap with audiobooks. While audiobooks can be a lucrative part of your backlist, they can be expensive to produce as an independent author. By selling the sub-rights, she keeps control over the formats that continuously make her money while tapping into an audience that she probably wouldn't have reached on her own.

As a hybrid author, it can be difficult to juggle all the different tasks involved in selling sub-rights for your book. You need to have a good understanding of the publishing industry and how it works, as well as an effective marketing strategy that will help to promote your book and drive sales.

Actionable Steps

Helen's analytical approach to publishing is fascinating for me, and the biggest piece of advice from her is to be smart about your choices, especially with more traditional contracts. Always bring a contract to a professional, whether that's your agent or a literary lawyer.

Having an experienced agent on board will help you navigate the publishing landscape and make informed decisions about how to market and promote your book. They will also be able to advocate on your behalf and connect you with potential partners or publishers for your sub-rights which can help boost sales and exposure for your work.

Pen Names

Most of the time, if you're currently in a contract with a traditional publisher, the language of the contract prevents you from publishing similar books to the ones that you have with them.

Competing titles from the same author usually aren't great for business in the traditional mindset. So, you may have to write in a different genre and find new readers.

Sometimes, this involves creating pen names to keep your books and readers separate, but this separation will help you gear your marketing to the right readers.

The biggest mistake that I've been course correcting for a few years now is publishing all my books, no matter what the genre under one author name. As more books revert to me and if I decide to indie publish them, I will be putting them under different pen names to segment my brand.

You can do so much with pen names, but it all depends on how much work you want to do. You could go as far as separating mailing lists, social media accounts, possible websites, etc. which all take extra time and sometimes money.

Money Mindset

If you're to make being an author a business, you need to put that business-publisher hat on regularly. As much as we are creatives, creativity doesn't die after you stop writing your book. Marketing itself is a creative career where you need to tell an audience a story to bring them into your fold. Sure, the point is to ultimately sell to them, but as authors, we have a leg up since we are usually natural storytellers. Don't discount this part of the process. If you intend to bring income into your life whether you are doing this full-time or part-time, you must change your mindset from, "oh, this is my book baby and I need to be precious with it," to something like, "how can I make this product lucrative for me?"

Rights reversion is a great way for traditional authors to gain back all or some of the rights to their books and re-publish them on their own or to leverage your publisher to market them more. I highly recommend tracking reversion periods and following up with your agent or publisher to review your options with your traditionally published backlist.

We've already seen the success of authors selling sub-rights, but it's worth mentioning again. Even if you are a KDP Select indie author, there are opportunities to sell print, audio, and foreign translations without breaking that contract.

Affiliate marketing within the indie-sphere is incredibly helpful to make even more from the sale of each of your books. This is a type of performance-based marketing in which a business rewards one or more affiliates for each visitor or customer brought by the affiliate's own marketing efforts. In the context of authors, affiliate marketing may refer to the practice of promoting and selling other people's books to earn a commission on each sale. This can be a profitable way for authors by using their platform to promote products they believe in. Currently, Amazon Associates, Apple Books, Google Play, and Bookshop.org offer these programs. Using your affiliate links in your books and content specific to each of those platforms will increase your revenue. To get started with affiliate marketing, it's important to first identify potential partners and opportunities that align with your interests and writing niche. This might include looking for relevant affiliate networks or websites that offer referral programs, as well as reaching out to other hybrid authors who have experience working in this area.

Another way to make money from our books is through the sale of merchandise related to our work. If you want to give your readers a fun way to show their support, there are many options available for selling branded products. You may want to consider working with graphic designers or artists to help create unique and compelling designs to really stand out. Or there are many options for the DIY approach, like Canva and Book Brush. If you are a traditional author, be sure you have permission to create items based on the books in your contract. Or work with your publisher on this type of project.

As hybrid authors, we know the importance of marketing our books and building a strong online presence. An effective way to do this is by writing regular blog posts, posting videos on YouTube, or launching a podcast. This way, we can connect with our target audience and showcase our expertise in a particular area or niche.

Outside of publishing books, there are many opportunities for writers to have author-adjacent methods of income, such as courses and workshops, freelancing, content creation, and more.

There is a huge demand for high-quality online content. There are numerous platforms available to help you create and market your course, including Udemy, Teachable, and Thinkific. Repurposing live or online workshops works in the same way where you can sell the course later if you have the rights to do so. Whether you're looking to speak at conferences, workshops, or local meetups, there are many opportunities for hybrid authors to share their knowledge and expertise with a larger audience.

Another way is to leverage our existing skills and expertise in other areas. This can include freelance editing, technical writing, and ghostwriting, all of which require specific knowledge and expertise that can be applied to a wide range of projects. Also, look into areas like cover design, project management, virtual assistant services, social media marketing, and more.

Making Your Backlist Work for You

You can leverage existing fans and followers on social media, utilizing book promotion services like BookBub, or even partnering with other authors to cross-promote each other's work. With social media, this can include sharing updates about new releases or promotions, engaging with readers through discussions or Q&A sessions, or creating promotional content around your book that fans can share with their own followers.

To maximize the potential of your backlist, it is important to start by identifying which titles might be best suited for marketing efforts. Some factors that you may want to consider include whether your book has performed well in the past (based on sales figures or reviews), whether it has a strong hook or unique angle that may appeal to a wider audience, and is part of a series or connected to other books in some way.

Even if you only have one book published, brainstorm ways you can leverage that book while you're writing the next.

I would suggest creating a reminder or recurring event in your calendar to review your backlist several times a year and think of ways that you can consistently keep the book in front of readers.

Case Study: Gail Carriger

Gail Carriger has published multiple New York Times bestsellers and has over a million books in print in dozens of different languages. She writes comedies of manners mixed with urban fantasy (and sexy queer joy as G. L. Carriger). She is best known for the *Parasol Protectorate* and *Finishing School* series. She was once an archaeologist and is fond of shoes, octopuses, and tea.

Initial Path to Publication

Gail started off traditionally published. I admire her author career and how it continues to ebb and flow throughout the years. With her start in 2008, she sold one of my favorite books of all time, *Soulless*, the first in *The Parasol Protectorate* series, and her first NYT bestseller which released in 2009.

Many authors I've spoken to who have gone hybrid have done so through the route of rights reversion. But Gail was savvy with her contracts and continues to sell so well in both indie and trad markets, around a 50/50 split, in fact! She expands her worlds with indie-published short stories and novellas, while publishing other books in genres that aren't currently favored by traditional publishers. Her fans are so incredibly loyal that they continue to support her, no matter what she publishes. This continues to bring new readers to her books.

Because I tend to "nerd out" over publishing things, I was astonished by how tight Gail's option clause was. The ability to continue to write what she wanted, give fans extra stories about side characters and shorter adventures that her publisher probably didn't want, or probably wouldn't know how to market, is genius. I'm still blown away, weeks after our conversation.

This is something to remember when faced with a contract. The option clause can be the death of an author name, which is why many authors have pen names to publish future books because of the "failures" of their past ones.

One of the biggest similarities Gail and I had was how many times we were "orphaned" with our publishers. Editors leave for many reasons, but most of the time, this comes out of the blue for authors and can be quite devastating. With your champion gone, you can either have someone else jump in with vigor to finish working on a book with you, or they can be lukewarm (and sometimes remiss) to work with you since they also have a workload from other authors. When this happens multiple times (at least in my experience), you will more frequently feel dejected because of the publisher.

Becoming Hybrid

With that catalyst, Gail spoke about a five-year plan to

flip her income from an 80-20 split with traditional as the higher to an 80-20 split favoring her indie books. After managing that, her next goal is to diversify her income through all of the wide platforms instead of a heavy dependency on Amazon sales.

One of the biggest takeaways from our conversation is that willingness to walk away. Especially with your debut, which you have most likely spent years on your book. To jump at the first iteration of the contract can be a foolish endeavor and bite you in the rear down the line.

I experienced this with my women's fiction contract where I wasn't willing to allow the publishers to control my film rights. My festive romance was my ode to Hallmark, and I'm obsessed enough with Christmas movies that I know networks are always looking for new content. Granted, it's a pipe dream, but when I'm able to keep most of the income, you bet your bottom dollar I'm going to do it.

As an author who also writes non-fiction for other authors, I'd be remiss not to mention Gail's publishing of *The Heroine's Journey*. To me, this concept was a huge revelation for my own writing journey, in how I tended to try to fit my stories into The Hero's Journey and then went off outline most of the time because it never quite felt right. But throughout Gail's academics in mythology and gender studies, she had the knowledge of both the hero and heroine's journeys. When she mentioned it at conventions, a lot of readers and writers wanted to know more. After writing the book, Gail showed it to her agent, and it was promising that she could get this book to an educational press, but hesitated. She thought of her reasons for why she wanted to get this book out there. That ultimately helped her decision to indie publish the book herself.

Income Diversification

Diversifying income is another huge plus of indie publishing because you don't have a publisher saying you can't. Gail has the typical formats such as eBook, paperback, and audiobook for her indie books, but also has a deal with a small press for limited omnibus, graphic novels, film deals, illustrated editions, jewelry, t-shirts, and has future ideas for recipe or crafting tie-in books, and coloring books. Her motivation when thinking about these options is what she would want to see from author's she loves, and that drives her thought process. Another recent example is her publishing a book only for sale on her website that included extras, deleted scenes, blog posts, etc.

She explained the "comet model" for independent creatives, where new releases are the flaming head of the comet, but most profit and career come from the long tail, reiterating her thought process of diversification of income, special editions of books, and continuously promoting her backlist. Being a wide author helps with a lot of these plans, and her decision comes with a responsibility to her fans as they have always been able to get her books where they want, due to starting in traditional publishing.

Gail is fortunate to have an agent who also works with a lot of independent authors and is open to attempting to sell foreign sub-rights for her indie books. Their healthy and more than a decade long relationship is a testament to how the industry can shift and move if it wants.

I find this an interesting conversation to pursue, because with both Rachael and Gail, literary agents, who tend to seem firmly placed in the traditional market, can achieve success while embracing the hybrid method. As an agent, you can stick with traditional, but by doing so, you are missing out on options for sub-rights, expanding your knowledge and "backlist" of projects, just like authors do.

Balancing Lists

The balance between having and not having control can be frustrating to most authors, and most of the time both sets of authors in traditional and indie experience this, but Gail takes a positive spin on it and experiments. For example, there was a hiccup with her books getting onto ACX (Audiobook Creation Exchange) and instead of succumbing to the anger and frustration of her fans asking when the book would be available, she offered the audio-book to them for a limited time until ACX had it available. I love how she continuously thinks of these frustrations as opportunities instead of limitations. It's a hybrid mind that will only benefit us as authors.

In terms of pitfalls, this one is super important for traditional authors going into the indie space. It's mostly Amazon's issue, but if you are in the US, it's important to file for copyright for your books, whether they are reverted or brand new. Your name is in a lot of different places in their algorithm, especially if you still have traditional books available from your publisher. This often will flag you within the system and they may take down your books or worse, your account.

Actionable Steps

Her biggest piece of advice for traditional, indie, and hybrid authors is to stay in touch with the industry, know comparative titles for your books, do the research on what is selling and how to market. Know the trends in the books themselves, but also cover art, formatting, platforms, distribution, and the like. This is imperative if you want to make this a career. Networking is super important to Gail. She's a part of several masterminds and has found her community through conventions. She recommends that you find authors who are a little further along than you or on the same level as this is where you find the most help when you need to whine or celebrate.

Carve Your Path

Whether you are an established author looking to expand your reach or a new writer looking to get started, being a hybrid author can help you achieve your goals and achieve success in the world of publishing.

This path can be overwhelming and scary, especially if you are not sure if you want to make the leap. However, it is important to remember that there is no right or wrong way to approach your writing career. By considering all the different options and opportunities available to you as a hybrid author, you can gain valuable insights into your strengths and interests, helping you find success no matter which path you ultimately choose. Whether you are looking to gain more control over your career or expand your reach to new audiences, ultimately, it comes down to finding what works best for you and embracing the challenges and opportunities that come with being a hybrid author. With determination, creativity, and the right mindset, there is no limit to what you can accomplish as a writer in this exciting and ever-changing landscape. So go out there and make your mark in whatever path you choose.

Author's Note

I almost didn't publish this guide in the way it needed to be written. There were and are a lot of aspects of the traditional publishing experience that I didn't like. I reached a tipping point of frustration with the lack of communication and control. Most of the time, I felt as if I was screaming into the void. If it wasn't for the incredible support system of some of the other authors at the imprint, I might have gone along with it, thinking that was the only way to be an author without looking at what seemed like at the time the wild west of independent publishing.

This guide was born out of negativity, but I don't subscribe to that feeling for too long in my life. I find that in painful moments, I seek to balance it out with something positive.

My frustration is with the traditional publishing system, not the editors, designers, and publishing teams who work for it. When I was able to separate the business from the people, I viewed the problem with more clarity. While it was difficult to turn down a two-book contract, I knew I couldn't keep going the way that I was. The traditional system favors a "money-first" mentality, which makes sense because it's a business. I implore you to keep this in mind when you put pen to paper on a contract.

As we continue to publicly challenge and unveil the mysteries of traditional publishing through the lenses of acquisition trials, bouts between bookstores and publishers, and authors who barely make enough money from advances to pay their bills, I strive to put advice and information out there based on an "Author-First" model. With independent publishing being an accessible and viable option for authors, a true competitor to traditional publishing, it is the way to our future where we make the choices for ourselves instead of someone doing it for us.

I understand some authors want nothing to do with independent publishing for many reasons, "Author-First" a mantra for you. It's a freeing concept that I quite enjoy and will continue to champion for.

Bonuses

This book has been all about knowledge and action to leverage your strengths as a hybrid author. So, take action now. To make it easy, I've provided all the resources mentioned in this book, full-length video interviews of the case studies, and a free starter workbook at:

www.katlynduncan.com/hybrid

Want to know more about rights reversion for your book?

Flip the page to read an excerpt from *Take Back Your Book: An Author's Guide to Rights Reversion and Publishing On Your Terms.*

Take Back Your Book

EXCERPT

Introduction

The dream for a lot of writers is to see their books on bookshelves. We want to spot readers posting beautifully curated photos on Instagram with glowing reviews and to hear how amazing our books are all across the internet.

That's all well and good, but, no pun intended here, books have shelf lives. Especially those published through a publishing house. The seasons of publishing with a large or small press turn over so quickly, and once your season has passed, then there's not much you can do for your book after that.

Or is there?

There are many clauses of a book contract that will affect your author career, but this guide is all about Rights Reversion.

Why?

It's a clause that can revive your book from the forgotten part of the shelf. Rights reversion allows you to grab that dusty baby of yours and clean it off for a whole new audience.

The best part is, you will finally take control over the entire process.

But I'm getting ahead of myself here.

Let's start with who I am, and why I'm so passionate about this topic.

My Journey

In 2009, I started taking my writing career seriously. I remember the moment my first book idea came into my head. I was walking through a parking lot and the story struck me like lightning. It was one of those unforgettable life-changing moments. I wrote this book during National Novel Writing Month (NaNoWriMo), which is an annual event held in November to finish a 50,000-word book within a month. I drafted that year, and several after, until I had a solid story. At this point, I was working full time in the medical field, and didn't put aside the time for my writing other than in November for a few years.

Shortly after NaNoWriMo 2012, there was a call for submissions for a new digital-first imprint of Harlequin UK. To caveat, I would never recommend submitting a book after NaNoWriMo, as most of the time a writer would have pushed through a first draft with little editing to "win". But this was my fourth iteration of the book, and it was in fairly good condition.

From that submission, the publisher reached out and I had a phone conversation with an editor. Ultimately, they loved the book and wanted a three-book series.

It was an absolute dream come true. I asked all the right questions, and it seemed like a perfect fit.

The three-book contract [Contract 1] landed in my

inbox, and I lived on Cloud Nine for weeks. I did my "due diligence" (notice the quotes here) and sent the contract to the lawyer who worked with us on selling our house (Mistake #1). I feel the winces and eye rolls. Hindsight is always 20-20. This lawyer did his best with the contract language, but as I came to realize, he didn't advise me of the nuances of a publishing contract, at least when it came to what exactly I was signing away. Proper knowledge about publishing is a must if you want to protect your books and career.

Fast forward to spring 2013, my debut novel, 'Soul Taken', the first in a series (*The Life After* series) of three young adult paranormal books, was out in the world. I was over the moon and had the debut author glow all the way through to the release of the last book in the series, which incidentally was less than a year later. Go digital-first publishing.

A note on digital-first publishing: This means the book will only come out in e-book to start. If the sales numbers skyrocket, the publisher may consider other formats (paperback, audio, etc.).

While I buried my head in drafting and editing the next two books, I thought everything would work out fine, because I had a publisher who was promoting my books (Mistake #2). If you don't already know, most publishers don't actively promote all the books on their lists the same. Unless you're a top title for the season, much of the promotion depends on you. Sure, there was the opportunity for social media posts and submissions to promotions that came later on (i.e. BookBub), but I had paid for my blog tour, book swag, and any other promotion for this series out of my pocket.

The next contract [Contract 2] came soon after, and my debut series would live on. Or so I thought.

My first brush with the idea of rights reversion was with the book I wrote while pregnant and then edited two months post-partum (again, digital-first publishing moves fast, but I would never recommend this for new parents because lack of sleep doesn't make a great book). It absolutely tanked within the first few months of release.

When I caught up with my editor about the next book in the series, she suggested I move in a different direction with my genres. Instead of giving up, I asked for promotions to bring the book in front of new readers but was told that maybe the book would have sold better if it was in a different genre.

I'll let that settle in for a second.

She said *my book might have done better* (the book that was already published) *if it was in a different genre* (even though this book had gone through edits as a paranormal novel). To say I was dumbfounded was an understatement. This advice should have been given in the editing stage!

Can you tell I'm still a little bitter?

There's no use writing a book like this without honesty. For reference, that novel has sold under one hundred copies in its lifetime. It's an absolute failure.

No doubt the editor realized that and swiftly encouraged me to write contemporary novels with a dark twist.

I had another book and novella in this contract, so there was nothing I could do but move on.

This is where my writer friends came to the rescue. I learned that this wasn't an isolated incident. Books that didn't hit the mark in sales were left to die at the bottom of the book charts, but no one loved those stories as much as we did. We wanted to see them thrive, but we had signed away all control. What could we do?

One of those lovely humans informed me about rights reversion. Immediately, I flipped open my contract and found that buried treasure. I contacted the contracts department with a request to return this book to me at once! (Mistake #3).

I swear I was nicer than that.

The contracts department sent me a reply that I wasn't even close to the threshold amount of years that the book could fall under consideration of reversion, so there was nothing they could do.

How dare they, right?

That is a rhetorical question. Here's the hard truth. I signed this contract. My signature bound these terms to me and my books. I had to move forward, knowing that this book would fail, and there was nothing I could do about it.

A year later, when my contract ended, my editor informed me that young adult was no longer an age range that they were publishing. Which, in hindsight, probably assisted my process of rights reversion.

My young adult option book idea was rejected, and its subsequent adult-alternative, so I was contract-free for a bit. This was disheartening, but I saw it as an opportunity to get an agent and continue publishing my young adult thrillers.

A few months later, a new editor at that same imprint emailed me, asking if I was interested in writing a book about mermaids, as they were the new trend. Up to this point, I had been ghostwriting for a few years, so I saw this as an opportunity to collaborate. They gave me a three-novella deal [Contract 3]. I hired a literary lawyer who pointed out clauses that I should work to get altered. The main contention points for me were the option clause and keeping audio rights. As an author with no agent, I had a lot of push back from the publisher.

With those emails filled with refusals to my requests, I felt ungrateful. They had given me the opportunity to write these books, so what right did I have to ask to keep some sub-rights and change clauses?

It was the wrong mindset, which I know now. Books take a lot of time to conceive, write, edit, and promote. With digital-first publishing, most authors don't get an advance, and with my contract, I didn't see any royalties until at least three months post publication.

I signed the contract, and from that moment through to publishing the third novella (this took about a year to get them all out), both editors who wanted the books in the first place had left the imprint. My champions were gone, and I was thrust upon other editors who weren't as passionate about these books.

Can you guess what happened? Those books, again, tanked.

That new contract meant a new option clause (which is an entire book in itself), but basically means that the publisher has first refusal to my next similar book. These differ wildly across the board, but mine wouldn't allow me to publish unless I gave them the book to check out first. As young adult was no longer an option, I gave them an adult Christmas novel that had lived in my head for years.

They offered another two-book contract [Contract 4], and as I'd built up enough confidence (finally!) I asked to retain film rights, as Christmas movies aren't in short supply and the royalty that I would have to split was too high for my comfort. Sure, this is a pipe dream, but why not? As I expected, they pushed back. But you know what? I had nothing to lose at this point. I knew enough about contracts that even if I gave them the option book, I could still refuse a contract.

No one was more shocked than me when they agreed to let me keep those rights. Finally, a win, right?

At that point, I was energized to take control. So, when the first book in my debut series came up for reversion, I took it. This winning streak didn't quit as they decided to revert the entire series (even though the second and third books' rights hadn't expired).

Now, I had three books that I had full control over. They were and still are the books of my heart, and I had to get them back into the world, but this time, under my terms.

Once the books were down from all the retailers, I had to make a plan. I've never self-published before, and I wanted to research what others did.

This time, Google failed me. Okay, the search engine didn't, but I couldn't find more than a handful of articles —most from five or more years prior—about what authors did after reversion.

Did they republish these books?

Drawer them?

Give them away for free?

What?!

I suppose the basic information about rights reversion in those articles hasn't changed, but I wondered if there was more to this story. I asked as many authors as I could what they did after reversion, but I still wasn't satisfied. My wonder took me on a deep dive for months about what I should do for this series, and then this book (yes, the one you're reading right now) hit me again like a lightning bolt, and I knew from past experience I couldn't let it go.

Lessons learned from my mistakes

- Always have a lawyer/agent who is familiar with literary contracts review a contract prior to signing.
- Understand that unless you are one of the top books of the season, you will have to promote your book in some capacity.
- When asking for reversion prior to the threshold, you better have a solid argument for those rights, or you will have to be patient.

What to expect from this book

- A brief overview of rights reversion, and how to ask for those rights.
- Options for your book after reversion.
- Monetary considerations of republishing.
- Considerations for your author career as an independent or hybrid author.
- Success stories from authors who have had their rights reverted.

Success stories

As I mentioned, there wasn't a lot of tangible information out there on other's paths after rights reversion. So, I did my own research, and that involved asking writer friends if they knew anyone who had been in my position before, and also scouring online author groups for threads discussing this topic.

I found a few, and they are mentioned in this book. I am beyond grateful to those who have taken the time to share their story to help authors in similar situations. My hope for these interviews is that you connect with a story and find inspiration to keep your books alive.

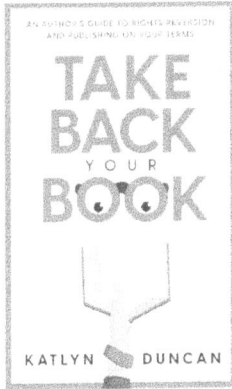

To continue reading, you can purchase the eBook and audiobook directly at:
www.katlynduncanbooks.com
or all formats from your favorite book retailer at:
www.books2read.com/takebackyourbook.

Acknowledgments

First and foremost, I want to express my sincere gratitude to Becca for the encouraging conversation that sparked the idea for this book. Without her support, this book would not have come to fruition.

I also want to thank Sacha, Julie, and Katie for being the best critique partners anyone could ask for. Your insights and feedback were invaluable in helping me to shape and refine the content of this book.

I am also deeply grateful to Gail, Rachael, and Helen for their contributions to the case studies and information about being a hybrid author. Their experiences and expertise added valuable depth and perspective to the book.

Finally, I want to thank all the hybrid authors out there who have inspired me and countless others with their hard work and determination. This book is dedicated to all of you and the success that you have achieved and will continue to achieve in the future.

About the Author

Katlyn Duncan is a multi-published author of adult and young adult fiction, and has ghostwritten over forty novels for children and adults.

When she's not writing, she's obsessing over many (many) television series', and hanging out on YouTube where she shares her writing process and all the bookish things.

Connect with Katlyn to order bulk copies or to inquire about speaking at your next event at

www.katlynduncan.com.

Also By Katlyn Duncan

Nonfiction

Take Back Your Book: An Author's Guide to Rights Reversion
and Publishing On Your Terms

The Successful Hybrid Author: Take Control of Your
Traditional and Independent Careers

Psychological Thriller

Her Buried Lives (as Katlyn L. Duncan)

Women's Fiction

Barefoot on the Beach

Wrapped Up for Christmas

Contemporary Fantasy

Secrets at Mermaid Cove

Young Adult Thrillers

Six Little Secrets

As You Lay Sleeping

Young Adult Paranormal

Soul Taken (as Katy Duncan)

www.ingramcontent.com/pod-product-compliance
Lightning Source LLC
Chambersburg PA
CBHW070026030426
42335CB00017B/2308